Hide
and
Seek

written by **Anne Giulieri**
photography by Ned Meldrum

You can play lots of *games* with your friends.

But one of the best games to play is hide and seek.

Look at the girls and boys.

They are at school.

They are going to play
hide and seek with you.

1, 2, 3, 4, 5, 6, 7, 8, 9, 10.

Look again!
Can you see
the boys and girls?
Where are they hiding?

You can play hide and seek outside with your friends too.

One of your friends can hide her *eyes*. Then she can *count* to ten.

You and your friends
can all run away.
You have to run very fast!

Look for a good spot to hide
in the *playground*.
It is not good for your friend
to see where you are hiding.

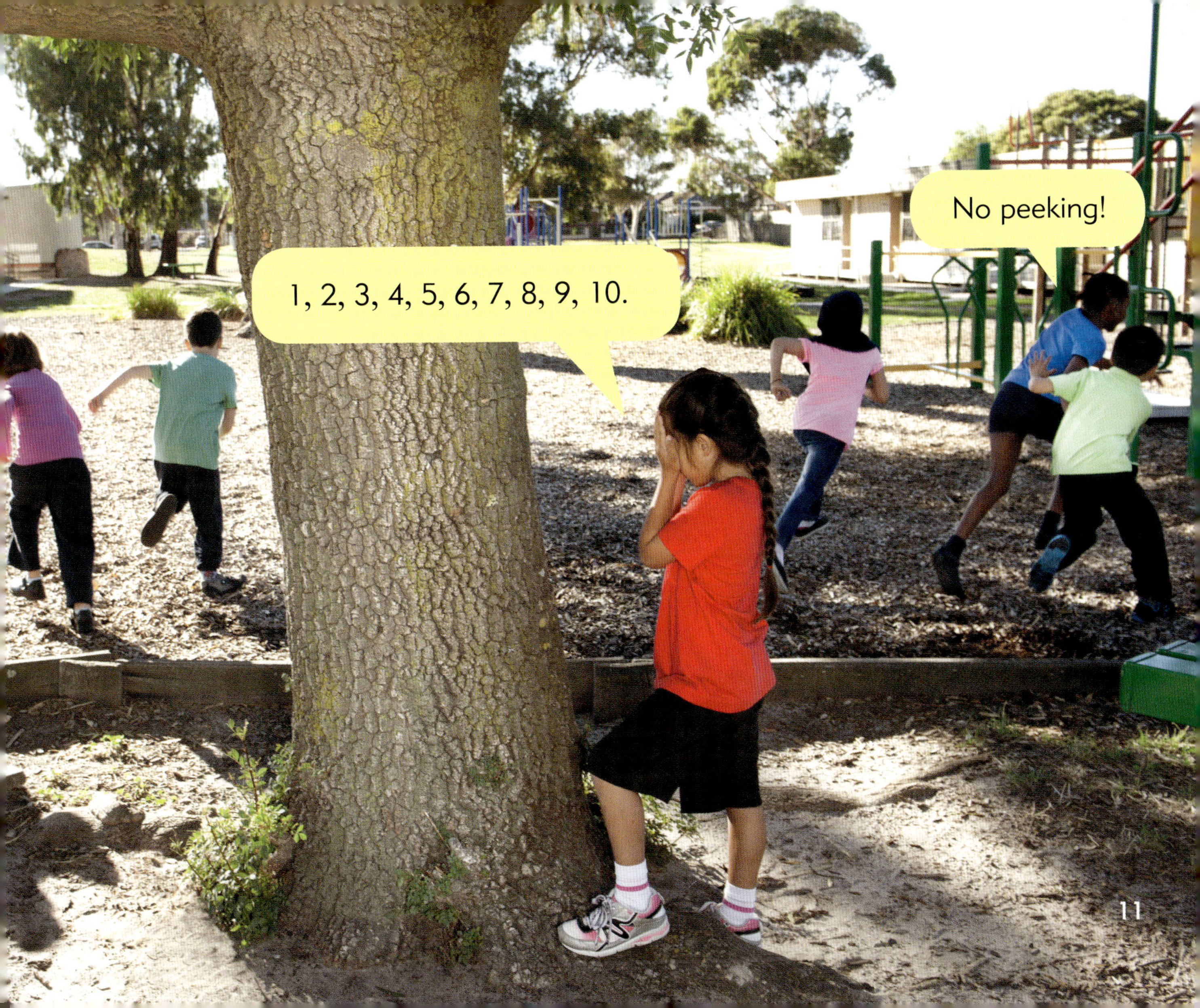
1, 2, 3, 4, 5, 6, 7, 8, 9, 10.
No peeking!

You can hide in the long *grass*,
or you can hide by a big tree.

You can hide by a log,
or you can hide
on the playground.

You can hide in the *tunnel*,
or you can hide in the *bushes*.
Shhhhhhh!

It is fun to hide.

Your friend will look for you.

But will she find you?

BOO!

Your friend can see you!

Picture Glossary

bushes

eyes

grass

tunnel

1, 2, 3, 4, 5, 6, 7, 8, 9, 10.

count

games

playground